IF FOUND, PLEASE RETURN TO :

NAME _____

PHONE _____

EMAIL _____

COUPONING BY STORE

SAVINGS BY STORE

STORE:

Date	Total Before Coupons	Total After Coupons	Total Savings	Notes

SAVINGS BY STORE

STORE:

Date	Total Before Coupons	Total After Coupons	Total Savings	Notes

SAVINGS BY STORE

STORE:

Date	Total Before Coupons	Total After Coupons	Total Savings	Notes

SAVINGS BY STORE

STORE:

Date	Total Before Coupons	Total After Coupons	Total Savings	Notes

SAVINGS BY STORE

STORE:

Date	Total Before Coupons	Total After Coupons	Total Savings	Notes

SAVINGS BY STORE

STORE:

Date	Total Before Coupons	Total After Coupons	Total Savings	Notes

SAVINGS BY STORE

STORE:

Date	Total Before Coupons	Total After Coupons	Total Savings	Notes

SAVINGS BY STORE

STORE:

Date	Total Before Coupons	Total After Coupons	Total Savings	Notes

SAVINGS BY STORE

STORE:

Date	Total Before Coupons	Total After Coupons	Total Savings	Notes

SAVINGS BY STORE

STORE:

Date	Total Before Coupons	Total After Coupons	Total Savings	Notes

MY WEEKLY COUPONING

COUPON SHOPPING LIST

WEEK OF:

Store	Item	Sale Price	Coupon	Total Saved	Total Paid

Store	Item	Sale Price	Coupon	Total Saved	Total Paid

NOTES / CALCULATIONS

COUPON SHOPPING LIST

WEEK OF:

Store	Item	Sale Price	Coupon	Total Saved	Total Paid

Store	Item	Sale Price	Coupon	Total Saved	Total Paid

NOTES / CALCULATIONS

COUPON SHOPPING LIST

WEEK OF:

Store	Item	Sale Price	Coupon	Total Saved	Total Paid

Store	Item	Sale Price	Coupon	Total Saved	Total Paid

NOTES / CALCULATIONS

COUPON SHOPPING LIST

WEEK OF:

Store	Item	Sale Price	Coupon	Total Saved	Total Paid

Store	Item	Sale Price	Coupon	Total Saved	Total Paid

NOTES / CALCULATIONS

COUPON SHOPPING LIST

WEEK OF:

Store	Item	Sale Price	Coupon	Total Saved	Total Paid

Store	Item	Sale Price	Coupon	Total Saved	Total Paid

NOTES / CALCULATIONS

COUPON SHOPPING LIST

WEEK OF:

Store	Item	Sale Price	Coupon	Total Saved	Total Paid

Store	Item	Sale Price	Coupon	Total Saved	Total Paid

NOTES / CALCULATIONS

COUPON SHOPPING LIST

WEEK OF:

Store	Item	Sale Price	Coupon	Total Saved	Total Paid

Store	Item	Sale Price	Coupon	Total Saved	Total Paid

NOTES / CALCULATIONS

COUPON SHOPPING LIST

WEEK OF:

Store	Item	Sale Price	Coupon	Total Saved	Total Paid

Store	Item	Sale Price	Coupon	Total Saved	Total Paid

NOTES / CALCULATIONS

COUPON SHOPPING LIST

WEEK OF:

Store	Item	Sale Price	Coupon	Total Saved	Total Paid

Store	Item	Sale Price	Coupon	Total Saved	Total Paid

NOTES / CALCULATIONS

COUPON SHOPPING LIST

WEEK OF:

Store	Item	Sale Price	Coupon	Total Saved	Total Paid

Store	Item	Sale Price	Coupon	Total Saved	Total Paid

NOTES / CALCULATIONS

COUPON SHOPPING LIST

WEEK OF:

Store	Item	Sale Price	Coupon	Total Saved	Total Paid

Store	Item	Sale Price	Coupon	Total Saved	Total Paid

NOTES / CALCULATIONS

COUPON SHOPPING LIST

WEEK OF:

Store	Item	Sale Price	Coupon	Total Saved	Total Paid

Store	Item	Sale Price	Coupon	Total Saved	Total Paid

NOTES / CALCULATIONS

COUPON SHOPPING LIST

WEEK OF:

Store	Item	Sale Price	Coupon	Total Saved	Total Paid

Store	Item	Sale Price	Coupon	Total Saved	Total Paid

NOTES / CALCULATIONS

COUPON SHOPPING LIST

WEEK OF:

Store	Item	Sale Price	Coupon	Total Saved	Total Paid

Store	Item	Sale Price	Coupon	Total Saved	Total Paid

NOTES / CALCULATIONS

COUPON SHOPPING LIST

WEEK OF:

Store	Item	Sale Price	Coupon	Total Saved	Total Paid

Store	Item	Sale Price	Coupon	Total Saved	Total Paid

NOTES / CALCULATIONS

COUPON SHOPPING LIST

WEEK OF:

Store	Item	Sale Price	Coupon	Total Saved	Total Paid

Store	Item	Sale Price	Coupon	Total Saved	Total Paid

NOTES / CALCULATIONS

COUPON SHOPPING LIST

WEEK OF:

Store	Item	Sale Price	Coupon	Total Saved	Total Paid

Store	Item	Sale Price	Coupon	Total Saved	Total Paid

NOTES / CALCULATIONS

COUPON SHOPPING LIST

WEEK OF:

Store	Item	Sale Price	Coupon	Total Saved	Total Paid

Store	Item	Sale Price	Coupon	Total Saved	Total Paid

NOTES / CALCULATIONS

COUPON SHOPPING LIST

WEEK OF:

Store	Item	Sale Price	Coupon	Total Saved	Total Paid

Store	Item	Sale Price	Coupon	Total Saved	Total Paid

NOTES / CALCULATIONS

COUPON SHOPPING LIST

WEEK OF:

Store	Item	Sale Price	Coupon	Total Saved	Total Paid

Store	Item	Sale Price	Coupon	Total Saved	Total Paid

NOTES / CALCULATIONS

COUPON SHOPPING LIST

WEEK OF:

Store	Item	Sale Price	Coupon	Total Saved	Total Paid

Store	Item	Sale Price	Coupon	Total Saved	Total Paid

NOTES / CALCULATIONS

COUPON SHOPPING LIST

WEEK OF:

Store	Item	Sale Price	Coupon	Total Saved	Total Paid

Store	Item	Sale Price	Coupon	Total Saved	Total Paid

NOTES / CALCULATIONS

COUPON SHOPPING LIST

WEEK OF:

Store	Item	Sale Price	Coupon	Total Saved	Total Paid

Store	Item	Sale Price	Coupon	Total Saved	Total Paid

NOTES / CALCULATIONS

COUPON SHOPPING LIST

WEEK OF:

Store	Item	Sale Price	Coupon	Total Saved	Total Paid

Store	Item	Sale Price	Coupon	Total Saved	Total Paid

NOTES / CALCULATIONS

COUPON SHOPPING LIST

WEEK OF:

Store	Item	Sale Price	Coupon	Total Saved	Total Paid

Store	Item	Sale Price	Coupon	Total Saved	Total Paid

NOTES / CALCULATIONS

COUPON SHOPPING LIST

WEEK OF:

Store	Item	Sale Price	Coupon	Total Saved	Total Paid

Store	Item	Sale Price	Coupon	Total Saved	Total Paid

NOTES / CALCULATIONS

COUPON SHOPPING LIST

WEEK OF:

Store	Item	Sale Price	Coupon	Total Saved	Total Paid

Store	Item	Sale Price	Coupon	Total Saved	Total Paid

NOTES / CALCULATIONS

COUPON SHOPPING LIST

WEEK OF:

Store	Item	Sale Price	Coupon	Total Saved	Total Paid

Store	Item	Sale Price	Coupon	Total Saved	Total Paid

NOTES / CALCULATIONS

COUPON SHOPPING LIST

WEEK OF:

Store	Item	Sale Price	Coupon	Total Saved	Total Paid

Store	Item	Sale Price	Coupon	Total Saved	Total Paid

NOTES / CALCULATIONS

COUPON SHOPPING LIST

WEEK OF:

Store	Item	Sale Price	Coupon	Total Saved	Total Paid

Store	Item	Sale Price	Coupon	Total Saved	Total Paid

NOTES / CALCULATIONS

COUPON SHOPPING LIST

WEEK OF:

Store	Item	Sale Price	Coupon	Total Saved	Total Paid

Store	Item	Sale Price	Coupon	Total Saved	Total Paid

NOTES / CALCULATIONS

COUPON SHOPPING LIST

WEEK OF:

Store	Item	Sale Price	Coupon	Total Saved	Total Paid

Store	Item	Sale Price	Coupon	Total Saved	Total Paid

NOTES / CALCULATIONS

COUPON SHOPPING LIST

WEEK OF:

Store	Item	Sale Price	Coupon	Total Saved	Total Paid

Store	Item	Sale Price	Coupon	Total Saved	Total Paid

NOTES / CALCULATIONS

COUPON SHOPPING LIST

WEEK OF:

Store	Item	Sale Price	Coupon	Total Saved	Total Paid

Store	Item	Sale Price	Coupon	Total Saved	Total Paid

NOTES / CALCULATIONS

COUPON SHOPPING LIST

WEEK OF:

Store	Item	Sale Price	Coupon	Total Saved	Total Paid

Store	Item	Sale Price	Coupon	Total Saved	Total Paid

NOTES / CALCULATIONS

COUPON SHOPPING LIST

WEEK OF:

Store	Item	Sale Price	Coupon	Total Saved	Total Paid

Store	Item	Sale Price	Coupon	Total Saved	Total Paid

NOTES / CALCULATIONS

COUPON SHOPPING LIST

WEEK OF:

Store	Item	Sale Price	Coupon	Total Saved	Total Paid

Store	Item	Sale Price	Coupon	Total Saved	Total Paid

NOTES / CALCULATIONS

COUPON SHOPPING LIST

WEEK OF:

Store	Item	Sale Price	Coupon	Total Saved	Total Paid

Store	Item	Sale Price	Coupon	Total Saved	Total Paid

NOTES / CALCULATIONS

COUPON SHOPPING LIST

WEEK OF:

Store	Item	Sale Price	Coupon	Total Saved	Total Paid

Store	Item	Sale Price	Coupon	Total Saved	Total Paid

NOTES / CALCULATIONS

COUPON SHOPPING LIST

WEEK OF:

Store	Item	Sale Price	Coupon	Total Saved	Total Paid

Store	Item	Sale Price	Coupon	Total Saved	Total Paid

NOTES / CALCULATIONS

COUPON SHOPPING LIST

WEEK OF:

Store	Item	Sale Price	Coupon	Total Saved	Total Paid

Store	Item	Sale Price	Coupon	Total Saved	Total Paid

NOTES / CALCULATIONS

COUPON SHOPPING LIST

WEEK OF:

Store	Item	Sale Price	Coupon	Total Saved	Total Paid

Store	Item	Sale Price	Coupon	Total Saved	Total Paid

NOTES / CALCULATIONS

COUPON SHOPPING LIST

WEEK OF:

Store	Item	Sale Price	Coupon	Total Saved	Total Paid

Store	Item	Sale Price	Coupon	Total Saved	Total Paid

NOTES / CALCULATIONS

COUPON SHOPPING LIST

WEEK OF:

Store	Item	Sale Price	Coupon	Total Saved	Total Paid

Store	Item	Sale Price	Coupon	Total Saved	Total Paid

NOTES / CALCULATIONS

COUPON SHOPPING LIST

WEEK OF:

Store	Item	Sale Price	Coupon	Total Saved	Total Paid

Store	Item	Sale Price	Coupon	Total Saved	Total Paid

NOTES / CALCULATIONS

COUPON SHOPPING LIST

WEEK OF:

Store	Item	Sale Price	Coupon	Total Saved	Total Paid

Store	Item	Sale Price	Coupon	Total Saved	Total Paid

NOTES / CALCULATIONS

COUPON SHOPPING LIST

WEEK OF:

Store	Item	Sale Price	Coupon	Total Saved	Total Paid

Store	Item	Sale Price	Coupon	Total Saved	Total Paid

NOTES / CALCULATIONS

COUPON SHOPPING LIST

WEEK OF:

Store	Item	Sale Price	Coupon	Total Saved	Total Paid

Store	Item	Sale Price	Coupon	Total Saved	Total Paid

NOTES / CALCULATIONS

COUPON SHOPPING LIST

WEEK OF:

Store	Item	Sale Price	Coupon	Total Saved	Total Paid

Store	Item	Sale Price	Coupon	Total Saved	Total Paid

NOTES / CALCULATIONS

COUPON SHOPPING LIST

WEEK OF:

Store	Item	Sale Price	Coupon	Total Saved	Total Paid

Store	Item	Sale Price	Coupon	Total Saved	Total Paid

NOTES / CALCULATIONS

COUPON SHOPPING LIST

WEEK OF:

Store	Item	Sale Price	Coupon	Total Saved	Total Paid

Store	Item	Sale Price	Coupon	Total Saved	Total Paid

NOTES / CALCULATIONS

COUPON SHOPPING LIST

WEEK OF:

Store	Item	Sale Price	Coupon	Total Saved	Total Paid

Store	Item	Sale Price	Coupon	Total Saved	Total Paid

NOTES / CALCULATIONS

Printed in Great Britain
by Amazon

79563073R00071